A BONUS MOM JOURNEY

PALMETTO
PUBLISHING

Charleston, SC
www.PalmettoPublishing.com

A Bonus Mom Journey
Copyright © 2022 by Jackie Lehrer

Hardcover ISBN: 979-8-8229-0470-5
Paperback ISBN: 979-8-8229-0471-2

A BONUS MOM JOURNEY

Weekly Reminders from 10 Years of Striving for Grace and Resilience

written and illustrated by
Jackie Lehrer

eing a stepmom can be an extremely confusing role. Having been one for 10 years, I was always wishing someone would give me sage advice or words of wisdom, but everyone I knew who was in a similar situation was just trying to keep their head above water as well. I created this illustrated book of weekly reminders that helped me move into a place of joy, ease, forgiveness and clarity when the bonus momming experience became overwhelming. It is my hope that they can bring you some peace as well.

Taking on the job of being a bonus mom is by far one of the hardest, loneliest, most emotionally taxing experiences you can have. There are so many different relationships and feelings swirling together into this strange mixing pot, and it's your job to find a place to exist inside of it. Some bonus moms enter the family dynamic with teenagers who can be extremely angry and difficult to connect with. Other bonus moms come into the picture when the family is young. Although that situation can seem easier from the outside, these moms mentally battle the reality that the kids aren't theirs. What's the best way to participate in raising bonus kids when they are physically with you, but also allow space for them to be raised completely differently at the other house? How does that dynamic show up in your family? In your marriage? Some family units thrive on open communication between the households, and there is space for both parties to parent together. But most blended families don't work that way, and issues with communication can cause a huge amount of stress and resentment. Whatever your situation is, it's certainly not easy. As a bonus mom, you get a unique perspective to see clearly what is happening with all the family relationships. You can see it all, you're living it all, but many times your hands are tied because you aren't the mom. How can you show up for everyone you care for in the midst of difficult bonus-momming situations but also create space to take care of your own needs? How can you do it without getting burned out? Answers to those questions take a lot of daily practice.

Before I met my husband, I had no idea what it meant to be a stepmom. I had no clue how much time and energy I would expend and the emotions that would be constantly triggered. I had no concept that our marriage would involve endless, looping conversations about what to do involving the kids or how to possibly get the ex-wife to communicate. I didn't know that for a period of time, these conversations would seem to take on a life of their own. I had no idea that I would have so many difficult, painful, infuriating discussions awaiting me or that I'd be dealing with lying and stealing while in a strange bonus-momming role. I didn't know I would spend a huge amount of hours researching schools and programs for the kids or spend just as many hours constructing written communication with my husband to the other household to hopefully get answers or a response or something. But I also had no clue the amount of love I would feel for these bonus kids.

I met my two bonus kids when they were both just barely six years old, at a perfect time in my life. As a childless thirty-year-old, I was used to enjoying my alone time, so being around them opened up a whole new chamber in my heart. I got to be silly, we played pretend games, and they held my hand. They filled me up in a way I had never experienced before. I loved doing things with them and hearing them call my name. I felt special and needed. My entire existence began to change. But as the days flew into months and years, life became more challenging. As much as I grew to love these little beings, I experienced firsthand how difficult being a bonus mom actually is.

In the early stages of being a bonus mom, I fantasized about stepfamilies that got along and raised the kids happily intertwined in the different households. I knew right away that wasn't our situation. Bonus momming proved to be extremely emotionally taxing, where I was constantly fighting upstream to find my place. Not knowing my role was a huge source of suffering for me. I

was a part of the family, so I should have a voice as well, right? I wanted to make a real difference. I wanted to contribute. I wanted to be someone the kids could trust. But the struggle of knowing how to do that in a space that wasn't easily defined was incredibly tough. There are no manuals on what to do as a bonus mom, and I made a million mistakes along the way. My intention was always to make the best of a tough situation, but it constantly felt like I was climbing a mountain just to do that. There would be another jolting comment by the ex-wife or a challenging conversation with a kid, or a feeling that I was being taken advantage of, and it felt like I was starting all over again.

The kids were being raised very differently than I would have raised them, and being the bonus mom, I just had to take a deep breath and roll with it. My goal was to love them as they were regardless of whatever was going on, but in the moment, what did that look like? How did this influence the way I should respond? It was hard when the kids' actions (or nonactions) affected me directly, and I was left not knowing what to do. Even if I felt that they should have learned this or that from their parents, I didn't want to teach them now. It wasn't my job…or was it? Was I here to step in and teach them things that I think they should know, or let them just show up however they chose, even if I felt it was disrespectful or not right? Many times I chose to do one thing only to realize that maybe I had made a mistake. One minute I was just the bonus mom, who of course wouldn't get a say in how the kids were being raised. After all, I wasn't the mom. So I really should be here only to play games and have a smiling face, right? But the next second, when they were at our house, and I was in the middle of obvious issues, what was my role then? When the kids were destroying some of my items, or didn't know how to use manners or apologize or make amends, or they were acting out because their needs weren't getting met—who was I then? Should I just keep my mouth shut and turn my head, or should I mother? When some of my items disappeared around the house, I kindly confronted them with hugs and a difficult conversation. That was mothering, wasn't it? Or when my bonus daughter was in tears and I held and rocked her—that was mothering as well. I know it was. Or when one of my bonus kids ruined a special item of mine and wouldn't admit what happened, I just wanted to scream and cry. But instead, I took a deep breath and sat with her and told her that she mattered more than this item and we would work through it as a team. That was being a mother as well. I realized in the midst of being a bonus mom, that yes, I wasn't 'the mom,' but I was a mom. And no matter

what, my goal was to support, love, connect, and see the kids the best that I could regardless of my title.

The other household was unavailable to discuss anything when issues showed up in the family dynamics. I felt so angry that my husband and I needed to parent alone. Making decisions based only on what we experienced when the kids were physically with us was extremely challenging and emotionally draining. The most difficult part of all of it was that my husband and I spent countless hours discussing the kids and the ex-wife and what to do and how to do it. We went in circles and only stopped because we were so annoyed and mentally shredded. It took over our marriage in many ways.

As the kids got older and we were able to interact with the ex-wife less and less, I started to feel more empowered. I created meetups for bonus moms in the area with the hopes of meeting like-minded, forward-thinking women, where we could all share some helpful tips and tricks that we have used to make life a bit easier. I met bonus moms at restaurants, in the back of dive bars, and inside cars. Many times they would burst into tears with stories pouring out of them. The details in the stories were unique, obviously, but the feelings and emotions were not. Everyone I met talked about feeling isolated, angry, disempowered, and unsure of their role. As difficult as it was to hear the specifics of other women's painful bonus-momming drama, I felt seen. Even though I didn't know them well, they understood why I felt so exhausted and angry. They got it. When it had been really hard, no one, not even my husband could relate to me. I would have loved to have a close friend who truly got what I was going through. Someone who could have said, "I've been there, and it's easier now. You can do this. I'm here for you in whatever capacity you need, but you will get through this, and it does get easier." Since I didn't have that, I imagined I'd be able to say it to someone who needs to hear it someday. That day is here. It does get easier.

Throughout my life, way, way before bonus momming was ever a part of it, I jotted down life lessons that occurred to me. Wherever there was anxiety, pain, fear, anger, sadness, or even the unexpected peace or joy, I would ask myself what the lesson was and write it down. So many times before I recognized the learning, my feelings were all over the place. But once I fully saw the lesson and was able to move through the feelings, they turned into these aha moments of clarity and inspiration. I learned there was always a nugget of knowledge to reflect on and allow me to alter the way I experience the world. Recording these snippets of learning has shown me that lessons are everywhere, in everything. The act of capturing life lessons is sacred to me. In many ways it has been like finding treasures along my path, each one unlocking a tiny part of myself that I didn't realize needed to be opened. When I acknowledge these learnings, I create a small gap of space to understand myself a little bit more, or forgive myself, or be at peace with who I am. Then, if it calls for it, I can take a step toward what I want, toward what feels right.

From the beginning of my ten-year bonus mom journey, I began writing down lessons for the same reason. I felt a strong sense of relief and empowerment recording them in the midst of all this difficulty. My favorite lessons that I've learned while bonus momming are in this book, *A Bonus Mom Journey: Weekly Reminders from 10 Years of Striving for Grace and Resilience*. These lessons give me energy, since I know I am absorbing, growing, and becoming in a deeper way. But here's the thing: I don't have these lessons mastered for myself. I wrote them from my highest, most ideal place, but that doesn't mean that I am there all the time. It is a practice just like anything. When I forget about them, I don't feel quite so empowered and strong. My goal has been to incorporate them into my daily life as a practice.

Making art, for me, has always been like taking a deep breath. It is another sacred process and my favorite form of meditation. Art is a place where I have learned to allow my mind to relax and my hand to move in whatever way it needs to move. I have developed a lot of trust in myself by not having a plan while I create. The freedom I have with my art has given me a template for having less of an agenda in many areas of my life. Like my art, I practice allowing life to just show up however it does and I do my best to ride waves instead of fight them. As I looked through all the lessons I had accumulated through the years, adding art to them seemed like the next logical step. I read the lesson, and let the art flow based on how the lesson felt in my body. The colors work hand in hand with the reminders to create a visual and emotional experience.

I have written and illustrated this book as a yearly flow, one quote per week for the whole year. There is space to curl up in them, practice them, and establish a true home with them. My hope is that you can incorporate these into your morning ritual and begin creating more of the feelings you want around yourself and your multidimensional family.

Love and light,

week 1

Being a BONUS MOM is a JOURNEY.
It is waking up Ready FOR a
FResh start, falling down,
getting Back up,
giving and taking, trying
a New dance,
meeting in the middle,
tripping, starting over,
seeing with clear eyes, and
embracing all areas of
light and dark.

1

week 2

ONLY I have
the POWER
to Make My life what
I WaNt it to Be.
I can do that
while Being a BONUS MOM.

3

week 3

when I show up
having taken care of me,
I am automatically
more accepting,
more fun,
and more heart-
centered every time.

5

week 4

Though sometimes I feel
unsure of my role,
I can go back
to the simple truth
that I am here
to love.
Love fully, love openly,
love with my whole heart.

7

week 5

It is Not
My joB
to Fix anyone.

9

week 6

I am practicing seeing
the kids as beautiful
lights, perfectly imperfect,
and loving them fully with
every ounce of me.
No matter what they are
doing, feeling, or experiencing.

week 7

It is my job to speak up and ask for my needs to be met.

13

week 8

I don't need the kids
to fill my cup.
My cup is filled by me first,
then my husband and friends.
I get my needs met elsewhere
so I can show up as a clean
slate with only love,
curiosity, and space
for them.

15

week 9

I am willing to dig
into the parts
of myself
that feel unlovable
and love them
anyway.

17

week 10

Everything
always works out.
It may not be the exact
timing I would prefer,
But everything eventually
falls into place.

19

week 11

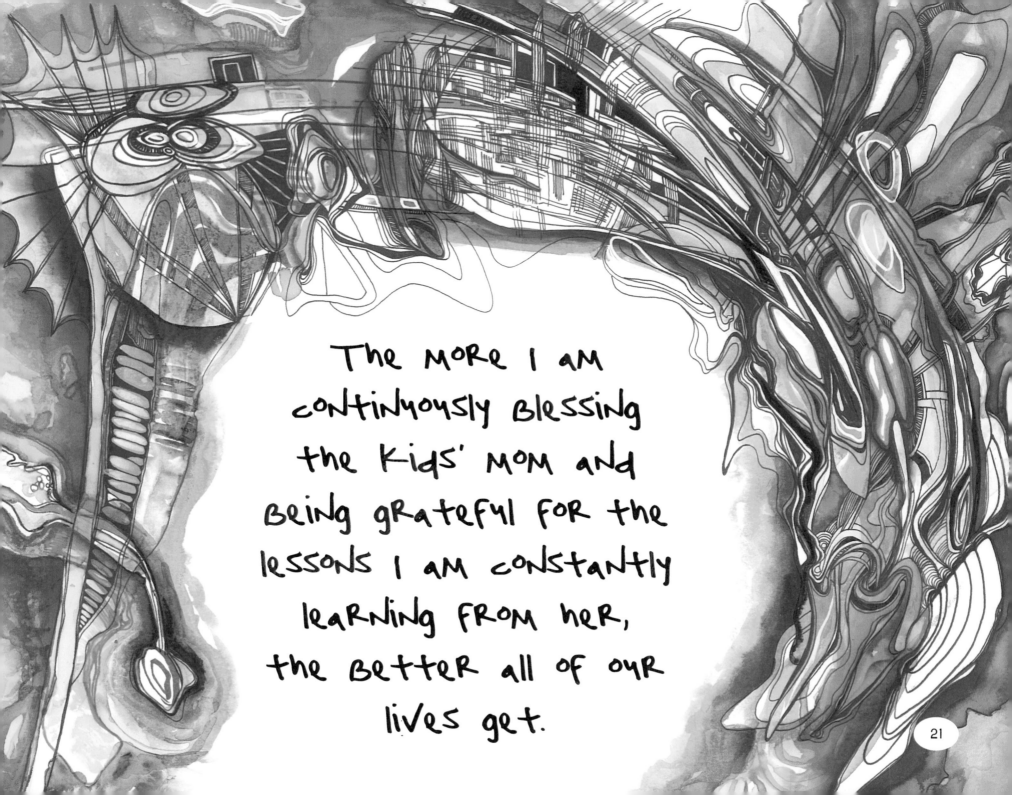

The more I am continuously blessing the kids' mom and being grateful for the lessons I am constantly learning from her, the better all of our lives get.

week 12

It is safe for me
to not be in control
of everything.
I can relax
knowing the universe
has my back.
I trust life.

week 13

I can love
myself
through the process
of BONUS MOMMING.

week 14

sometimes
I have to say to myself,
"I give you permission
to feel
everything you need
to feel."

27

week 15

I don't Need to always Be easygoing, and Playful. Sometimes I am FRUStRated, angRy, and Sad. These feelings are just as valid and Need to Be hoNoRed.

29

week 16

When I show up
in my truth,
I have more
power
than I realize.

week 17

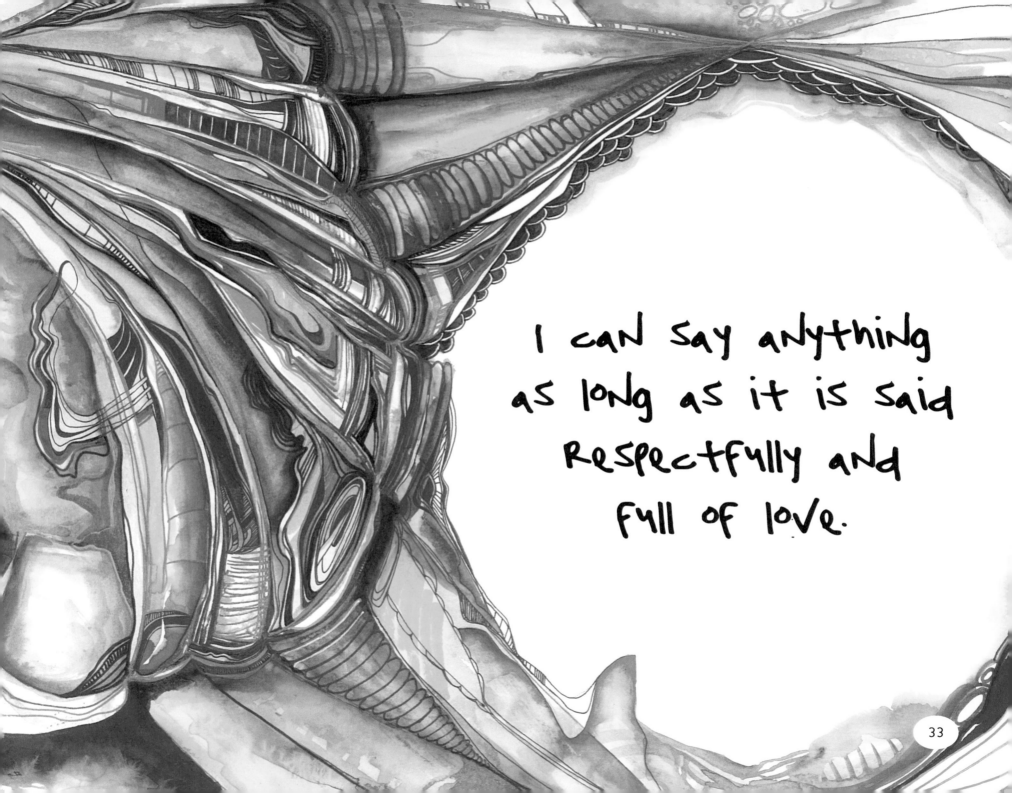

I can say anything as long as it is said Respectfully and full of love.

week 18

Whatever situations my husband came from in his previous marriage allow him to show up better for me. I can remember this!

week 19

IF I can Be
MoRe gentle
with myself,
I can Be
MoRe gentle
with otheRs.

37

week 20

When it comes to
dealing with the other household,
I'm learning to make choices
that are easiest for me,
my relationship with my
husband,
and my inner peace.
That is my focus.

39

week 21

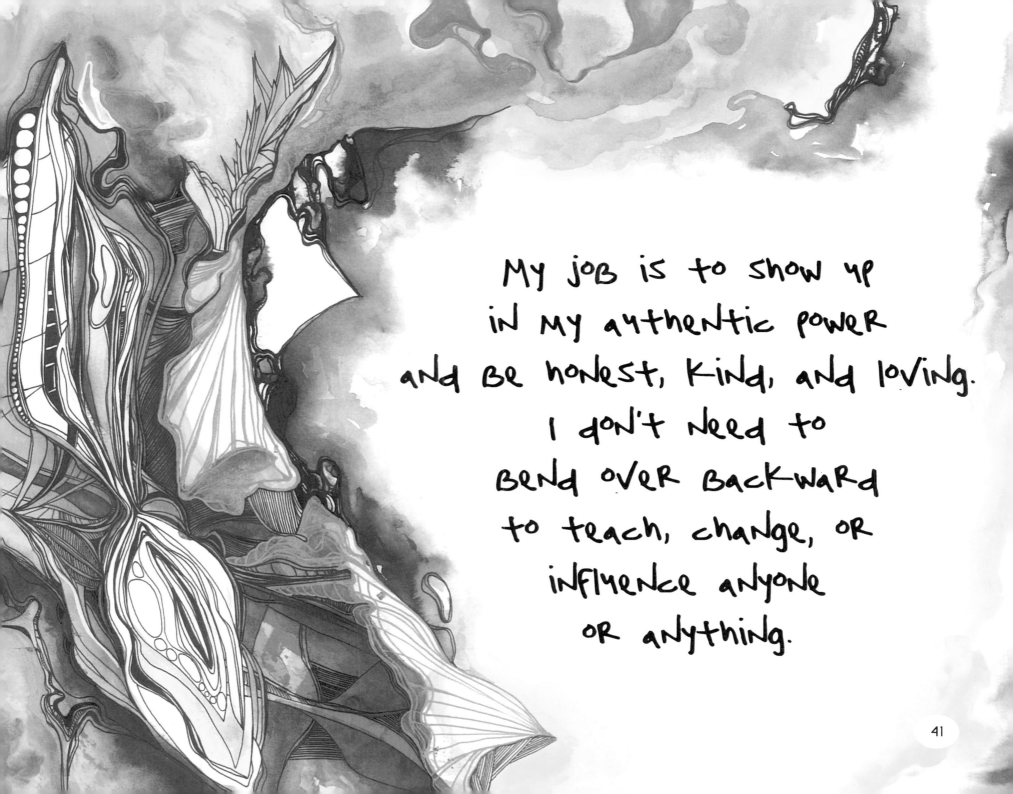

My job is to show up
in my authentic power
and be honest, kind, and loving.
I don't need to
bend over backward
to teach, change, or
influence anyone
or anything.

week 22

I offer a different personality,
perspectives, and experiences
than their mom.
The kids get an opportunity
to see the way
another woman views life.
What a gift!

week 23

BONUS MOMMING IS
BREAKdowns,
BREAK OPENS,
and BREAKthroughs.

45

week 24

Just when things feel dark,
an unexpected gift appears
and reminds me that I am
exactly where I'm supposed to Be.
It may Be a smile,
the sharing of a laugh,
or a sweet little note.
This happens when I need it
the most.

47

week 25

For just a moment
at a time,
I see everything
through a lens
of love.

49

week 26

I can remember
as often as possible
that these kids are my
greatest teachers,
and that there is
always a new lesson
for me to learn about
myself, life, love, and
connection.

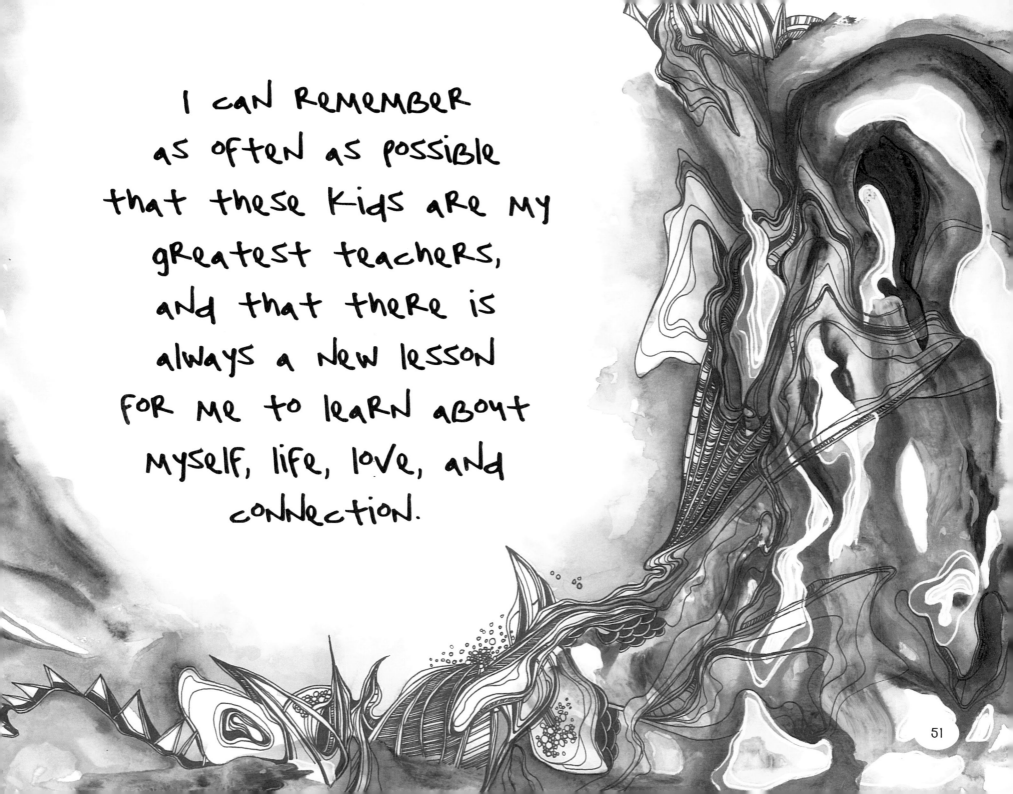

week 27

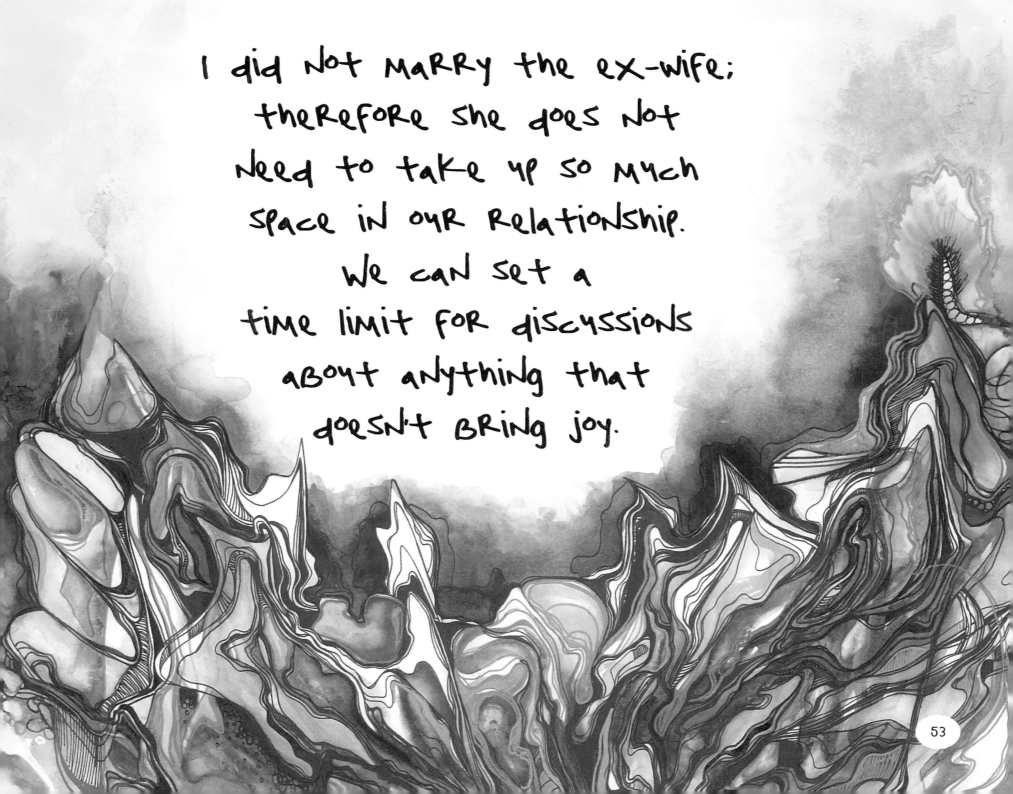

I did not marry the ex-wife;
therefore she does not
need to take up so much
space in our relationship.
We can set a
time limit for discussions
about anything that
doesn't bring joy.

53

week 28

Love
is a choice
that I choose
again
and again.

55

week 29

Even in a
single moment,
I can make a difference.
A moment of asking
questions, making
eye contact,
and showing that I care.
Every moment counts!

week 30

I can meet the kids
as they are with
all my love.
I do not need them
to be different
for me to love
them fully.

week 31

I can choose to
find peace
in small moments.

week 32

I don't need to concern
myself
with what the kids' mom is
learning or
how she is growing.
My job is to stay in my
own lane
and learn the many lessons
that are here for me.

week 33

THeRe is always something New to leaRN.

week 34

My feelings, my thoughts,
and my fears matter.
It is up to me to
speak my truth.
These kids can learn
and grow
from witnessing
vulnerability.

week 35

The First thought of what
to do is usually the most
authentic answer.
I can choose to act
more often from that First
gut Feeling
and trust that my
intuition is
always guiding me.

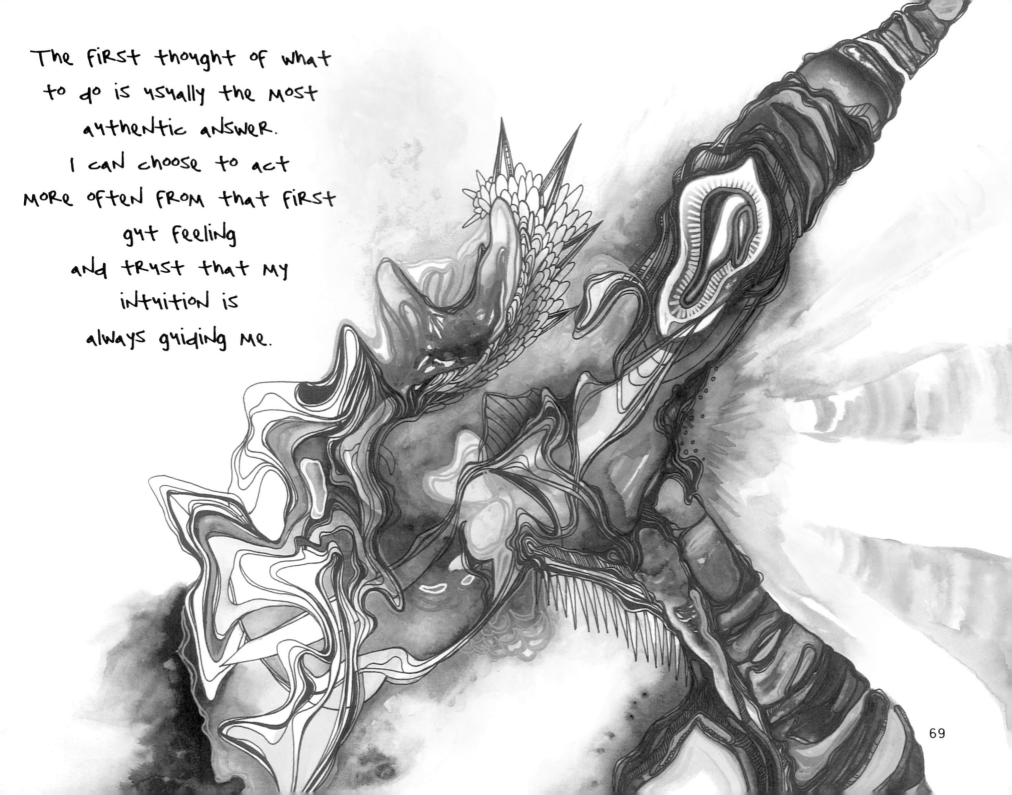

week 36

I focus on the things I have control over: feeling my feelings, being kind and having boundaries.

week 37

Having alone time
with each Kid,
where my attention is
and completely on them,
strengthens our Bond and
plants seeds of connection.
This is one of the
most important things
I can do.

73

week 38

spending more of my
energy
acknowledging things
I appreciate
about all members of
my family
is the quickest way
to feel closer to them.

week 39

Sometimes I whisper,
"I forgive you,
I forgive you,
I forgive you..."
Directing the forgiveness
to my husband,
to my bonus kids,
to traffic,
But usually, and most importantly,
to myself.

week 40

I'M willing to let life take the twists and turns it needs to get me to where I want to be.
I can be flexible with life.

79

week 41

These Kids were
Raised differently
than how I would have
Raised them.
It's okay to feel
FRustRated.
I can still choose
to love them
as they are.

81

week 42

sometimes
the anger I think I'm feeling
toward my BONus kids or
the other household
is really anger I have
toward my husband.
It is safe to acknowledge this,
feel it all the way through,
and then release.

83

week 43

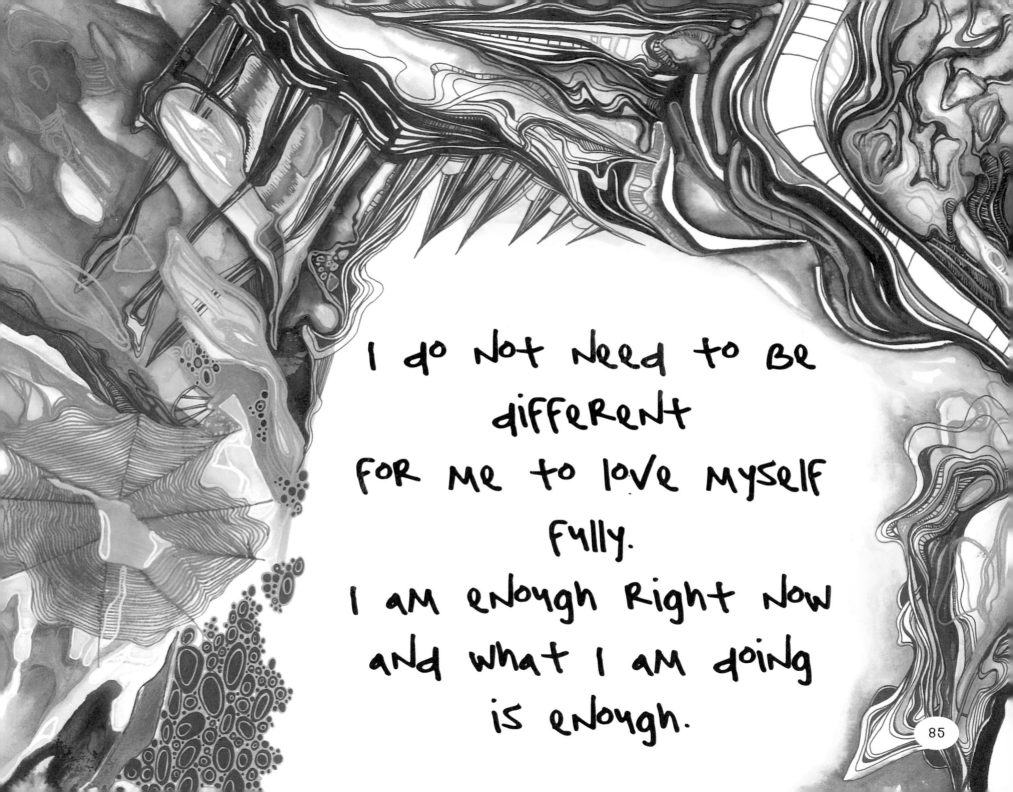

I do Not Need to Be
diffeRent
foR Me to love Myself
fully.
I aM eNough Right Now
and what I aM doing
is eNough.

85

week 44

Vulnerability is scary,
even for an adult.
But I choose to do it
anyway,
trusting that it's always
the pathway to
deeper Relationships.

week 45

To fully embrace
my role of being a
bonus mom,
I have a choice every moment
to engage or not engage.
It is a choice
to show up as my truest self
or not.
It is a decision every day
to say yes.

week 46

When things get difficult
with the kids,
I can choose to REMEMBER
that I have the power
to show up as my
highest self.
I can REMEMBER to
Be compassionate
and loving
while still
Being honest.

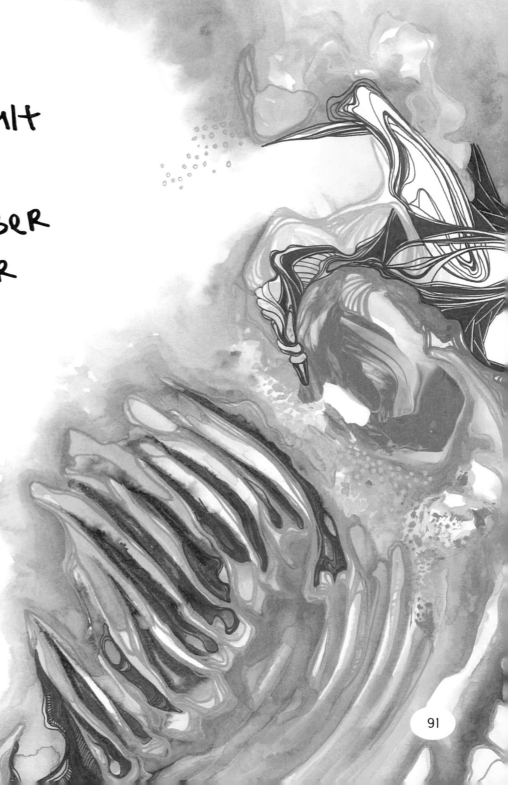

week 47

Sending love
to the ex-wife
(when I'm in the
mental space
to do it)
Makes me feel good.
Everyone benefits
from love.

week 48

Going away to take
care of me
and preserve my
energy
is sometimes the
best decision
I can make.

95

week 49

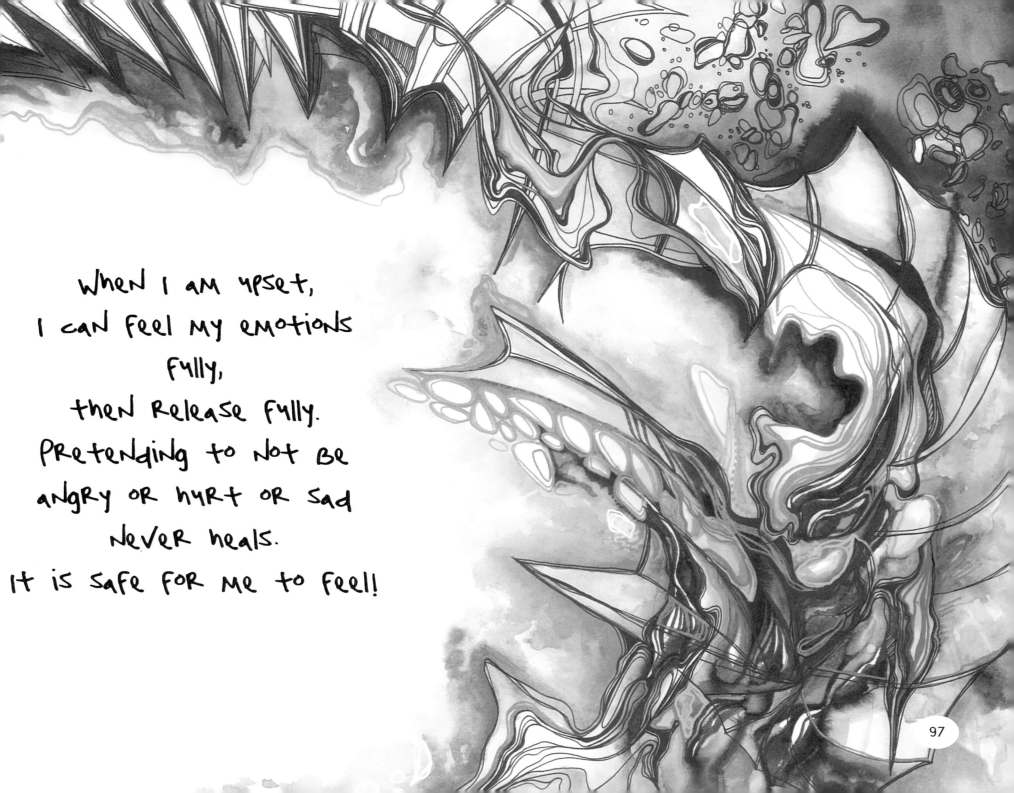

When I am upset,
I can feel my emotions
fully,
then Release fully.
Pretending to Not Be
angry or hurt or sad
Never heals.
It is safe for me to feel!

week 50

Anger is a signal that needs to be listened to. It shows me instantly what isn't working. I can choose to pay attention to my anger, to respect it, and to make changes accordingly.

week 51

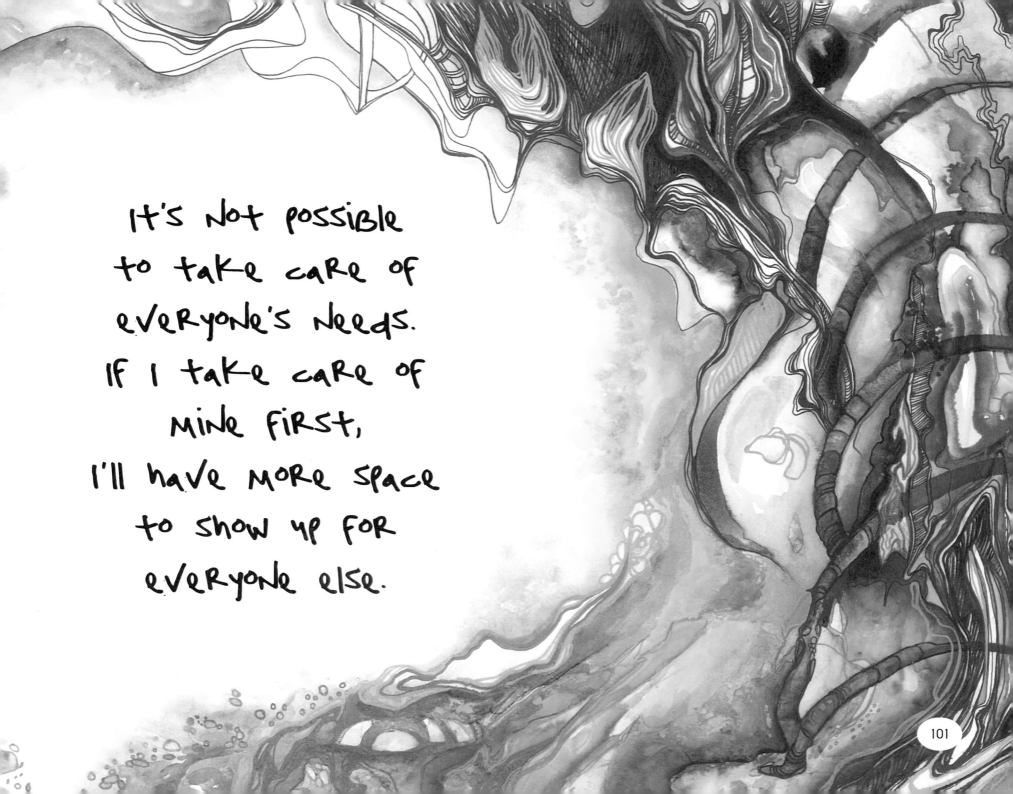

It's not possible
to take care of
everyone's needs.
If I take care of
mine first,
I'll have more space
to show up for
everyone else.

week 52

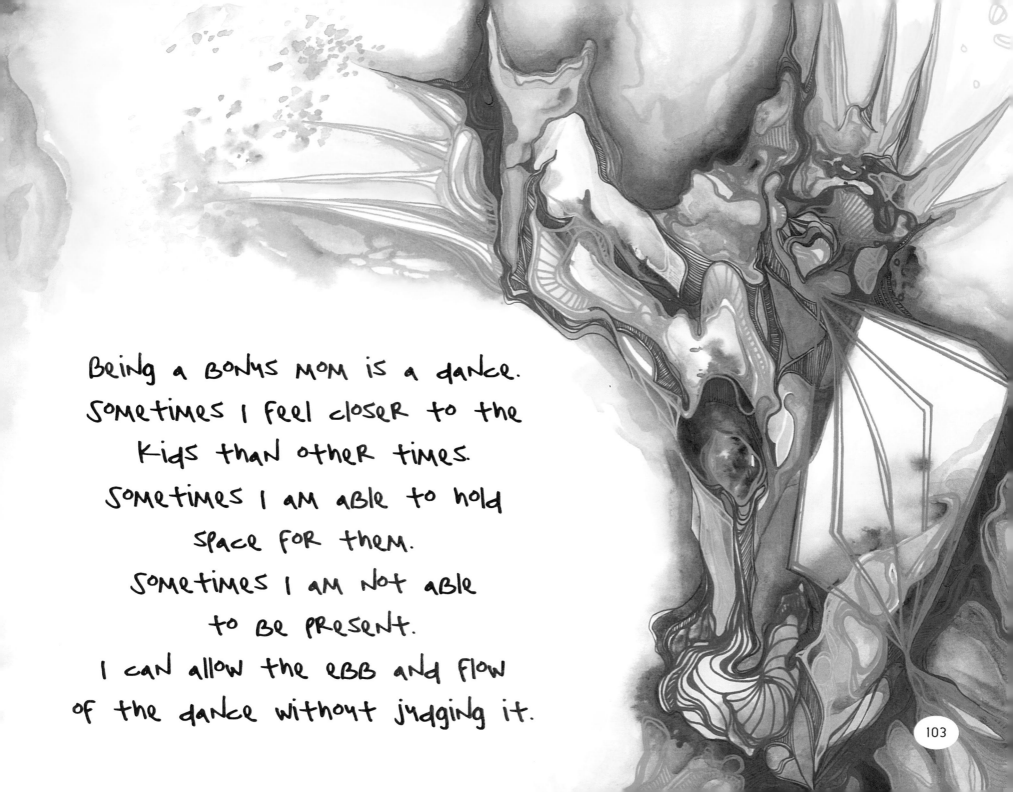

Being a Bonus Mom is a dance.
Sometimes I feel closer to the
kids than other times.
Sometimes I am able to hold
space for them.
Sometimes I am not able
to be present.
I can allow the ebb and flow
of the dance without judging it.

103

About the Author

Jackie Lehrer is an artist and creator. She is a collector of lessons and seeker of knowledge and joy. When not making art, she enjoys yoga, baking, family time, and her husband's amazing culinary skills. She lives in San Diego with her husband, daughter and 2 bonus kids.

Ingram Content Group UK Ltd.
Milton Keynes UK
UKRC030908280323
419046UK00003B/1